First Facts®

Amazing Animal Architects

AMAZING Animal Architects

by Yvonne Pearson, Rebecca Rissman and Mari Schuh Quam

raintree

a Capstone company — publishers for children

Raintree is an imprint of Capstone Global Library Limited, a company incorporated in England and Wales having its registered office at 264 Banbury Road, Oxford, OX2 7DY – Registered company number: 6695582

www.raintree.co.uk
myorders@raintree.co.uk

Edited by Karen Aleo
Designed by Sarah Bennett
Picture research by Morgan Walters
Original illustrations © Capstone Global Library Limited 2018
Production by Tori Abraham
Originated by Capstone Global Library Limited
Printed and bound in India

ISBN 978 1 4747 6822 1
22 21 20 19 18
10 9 8 7 6 5 4 3 2 1

British Library Cataloguing in Publication Data
A full catalogue record for this book is available from the British Library.

Acknowledgements
We would like to thank Professor James L. Gould of the Department of Ecology and Evolutionary Biology at Princeton University and Carol Grant Gould for their invaluable help in the preparation of this book.

We would like to thank the following for permission to reproduce photographs: Shutterstock: chakkrachai nicharat, 27, Chase Dekker, Cover, Chutima Chaochaiya, (blueprint) design element throughout, CRS PHOTO, 11, Janos Rautonen, 7, Kristel Segeren, 21, Peter Hermes Furian, (map) design element throughout, Pong Wira, 15, Remoau, 5, Salparadis, 13, SARAWUT KUNDEJ, 29, sauletas, 19, Viktor Loki, 25, Vishnevskiy Vasily, 9, Wang LiQiang, 20, Zoltan Tarlacz, 17; Wikimedia: Zoë Helene Kindermann, 23.

Every effort has been made to contact copyright holders of material reproduced in this book. Any omissions will be rectified in subsequent printings if notice is given to the publisher.

Contents

Amazing builders

Animals build some amazing homes! Some animals gather grass, stones and sticks. Other animals make building materials inside their bodies. One animal uses its own body as the building material!

The homes they build keep the animals and their young safe. They can help protect the animals from **predators**.

predator animal that hunts other animals for food

Coots build their nests in shallow water.

Sociable weavers

Hundreds of **sociable** weavers share a bird's nest that looks like a haystack. Just one nest can have more than a hundred chambers. A pair of birds lives in each chamber.

The birds use sticks to make a roof that keeps out rain and sunshine. Soft grass and fur fill the chambers. Spiky straw is used for the entrances to keep out snakes.

sociable tending to live in groups or packs

WHERE SOCIABLE WEAVERS LIVE

Sociable weavers build in trees with long trunks and high branches. These trees make it hard for predators to reach the nest.

RANGE MAP

Paper wasps

Paper wasps make nests from chewed wood and **saliva**. The **queens** and other female wasps scrape off wood from trees and fence posts. They chew the wood and mix it with their saliva to make **pulp**. The wasps make **cells** in the nest. These spaces hold their eggs. The pulp turns into paper when it hardens and dries.

saliva liquid in the mouth

queen adult female wasp or other insect that lays eggs

pulp mixture of ground-up paper and water

cell small space; one of the spaces in a paper wasp nest is a cell

WHERE PAPER WASPS LIVE

Paper wasps live in covered areas such as under tree branches and porch roofs.

RANGE MAP

Baya weavers

Male baya weavers use blades of grass and palm leaves to make their nests. The bird **weaves** the pieces together with its beak and claws. Then it adds a long **tunnel** to the nest. The bird uses the tunnel to enter its home. Predators cannot get inside.

weave pass grass, sticks and other materials over and under one another to make a nest

tunnel narrow passageway

WHERE BAYA WEAVERS LIVE

Baya weavers build nests in trees. They look for branches that hang over water.

RANGE MAP

FACT

Male baya weavers use their nests to attract mates.

Leaf-cutter ants

Leaf-cutter ants dig tunnels and chambers that stretch deep into the ground. The ants use the chambers to raise their young. But that's not all.

The ants are skilled gardeners. They bring pieces of leaves to the nest. They use the leaves to grow a **fungus**. Then the ants eat the fungus.

fungus living thing similar to a plant, but without flowers, leaves or green colouring; fungi are a group of organisms that include mushrooms

WHERE LEAF-CUTTER ANTS LIVE
Leaf-cutter ants build their nests in rainforests.

RANGE MAP

Trapdoor spiders

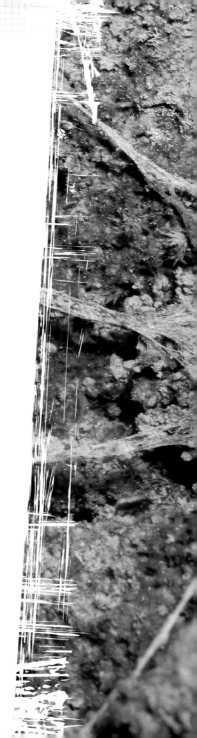

A spider waits in its hidden burrow. A cricket comes close. The spider bursts through a trapdoor. It drags the **prey** inside to eat it.

Trapdoor spiders make underground burrows. They line their burrows with silk, saliva and soil. Most trapdoor spiders make a door for the burrow opening. The trapdoor swings on a **hinge** and is **camouflaged**. This makes the burrow hard to see.

prey animal hunted by another animal for food

hinge moveable part where two things are connected

camouflage made to blend in with the things around it

WHERE TRAPDOOR SPIDERS LIVE
Trapdoor spiders burrow in warm grassy areas, hillsides or riverbanks.

RANGE MAP

FACT
Some types of trapdoor spiders use strings of silk to tell them when prey is near. When the prey touches the silk, the spider feels the string move. It rushes out to catch the prey.

15

Prairie dogs

Many prairie dogs live in big groups called towns. They work together to dig underground homes. They use their strong paws and sharp claws to dig tunnels, chambers and openings. Some chambers are used for raising their young. Others are used for sleeping or storing waste.

Prairie dogs aren't the only ones using their burrows. Ferrets and other small animals sometimes crawl in too.

FACT

A 40,234-square kilometre (25,000-square mile) prairie dog town was once discovered in Texas, USA. About 400 million prairie dogs lived there.

WHERE PRAIRIE DOGS LIVE
Prairie dog towns can be found in open grasslands. A mound of packed soil is often at the burrow entrance.

RANGE MAP

Eastern moles

Dig, dig, dig. A mole is at work! Eastern moles live mainly below the ground. They have wide front paws and sharp claws. They use them to dig shallow, twisting tunnels. This is where they find insects to eat. They also dig deeper tunnels that lead to chambers. The moles use these areas to rest, store food and raise their young.

WHERE EASTERN MOLES LIVE
As moles dig, they push the extra soil out of their tunnels onto the surface. These form small mounds called molehills.

RANGE MAP

FACT
Animals called gophers are sometimes mistaken for moles. But a mole has a long snout and tiny eyes. Gophers have shorter snouts and long front teeth.

Montezuma oropendolas

Near the Caribbean Sea, gold-tailed birds make hanging nests in rainforest trees. These nests look like drooping sacks. The long nests stop eggs falling out when the wind blows.

Females weave the nests on tall trees that are away from other trees. Then monkeys and other predators can't grab the eggs.

WHERE MONTEZUMA OROPENDOLAS LIVE

Montezuma oropendolas build nests in large trees that are not near other trees.

FACT
More than 100 nests can hang from one tree.

Hazel dormice

This is a hazel dormouse curled up in its tiny nest.

Hazel dormice weave tiny, ball-shaped nests. They **hibernate** in these nests during the cold winter months. The outside of the nest is made of woven sticks, leaves and bark. The inside is lined with feathers, moss and grass. The mice use their sticky saliva to help hold the nest together.

hibernate spend winter in a deep sleep; animals hibernate to survive low temperatures and lack of food

FACT
During the summer, hazel dormice often make different nests. They are slightly larger and usually found in low branches of trees or bushes.

In winter, dormice nests are found under piles of leaves or near logs.

RANGE MAP

Beavers

How do beavers build their homes? Many start by building a **dam**. The beavers gnaw trees until they fall across streams. Then they pile branches, stones and mud on the trees.

A dam helps to make a pond still and safe for a beaver's **lodge**. The beavers build their lodges with wood, stones and plants. They use mud to make their homes waterproof.

dam barrier built to block a body of water

lodge beaver's home of mud, logs and sticks, built in water

WHERE BEAVERS LIVE

Beaver dams are found in freshwater ponds and rivers. Beavers build lodges close to the dams.

RANGE MAP

lodge

dam

Fire ants

When there's a flood, fire ants keep their queen and larvae safe. They build rafts by linking their bodies together. In this way, they make sure their **colony** survives. They trap air bubbles to help them float. A material like wax helps to keep them dry.

Fire ants can attack humans and animals. The ants have strong stings and powerful jaws.

colony large group of insects that live together

WHERE FIRE ANTS LIVE

Fire ants build mounds in sunny places. After a lot of rain, fire ants may be found floating in water.

RANGE MAP

Corals

Coral reefs look like colourful underwater castles. They are really the **skeletons** of tiny **polyps**.

Each polyp makes a hard skeleton shaped like a cup. The polyp sits inside the cup to stay safe. Many polyps group together and form a reef.

skeleton bones that support and protect the body of a human or other animal

polyp small sea animal with a tube-shaped body

WHERE CORALS LIVE

Corals are found on the sandy bottoms of warm oceans.

RANGE MAP

FACT

Corals are very important. They give shelter to a quarter of all ocean life.

Glossary

camouflage made to blend in with the things around it

cell small space; one of the spaces in a paper wasp nest is a cell

colony large group of insects that live together

dam barrier built to block a body of water

fungus living thing similar to a plant, but without flowers, leaves or green colouring; fungi are a group of organisms that include mushrooms

hibernate spend winter in a deep sleep; animals hibernate to survive low temperatures and lack of food

hinge moveable part where two things are connected

lodge beaver's home of mud, logs and sticks, built in water

polyp small sea animal with a tube-shaped body

predator animal that hunts other animals for food

prey animal hunted by another animal for food

pulp mixture of ground-up paper and water

queen adult female wasp or other insect that lays eggs

saliva liquid in the mouth

skeleton bones that support and protect the body of a human or other animal

sociable tending to live in groups or packs

tunnel narrow passageway

weave pass grass, sticks and other materials over and under one another to make a nest

Find out more

The Animal Book: A Visual Encyclopedia of Life on Earth, DK (DK Children, 2013)

Look Inside a Burrow (Look Inside), Richard Spilsbury (Raintree, 2013)

What Can Live in a River? (What Can Live There?), John-Paul Wilkins (Raintree, 2014)

Learn more about one of the most amazing animal architects at: **www.bbc.co.uk/nature/life/Beaver**

Find out more about coral reefs at: **www.dkfindout.com/uk/animals-and-nature/habitats-and-ecosystems/coral-reef**

Index